Manuel's Day Out

MANUEL'S MISSIONS Series

BOOK SIX

Written by Warren Ravenscroft
Illustrations by Zoe Jones

Guiding and Leading.

Psalm 23:1-3

Ah! That was a wonderful sleep, thought Manuel as he stretched his little body to greet a new day. Manuel made his way from his bed next to the warm fire in the lounge room, to the kitchen.

As he sleepily crept to his breakfast plate, he heard
a quiet voice say, "Good morning sleepyhead. You
are late this morning." It was Mary who spoke as
she busily placed the dishes in the cupboard.

When Manuel had finished eating, he thought, *I'll go to the front porch and sit with George while he reads the paper. I am sure there is a lovely warm sunny spot where I can lie.* He scurried down the hallway and out onto the verandah. The morning paper was still wrapped up sitting on the table. *Where is George?* thought Manuel, *he always reads the morning paper!*

Manuel returned to the kitchen as Mary placed two freshly baked biscuits on a plate next to a mug of coffee. She looked at Manuel, "He's not reading today, Manuel, so let's go and see what George is up to." Manuel was not only mischievous, but an inquisitive little mouse and he didn't need a second invitation, so he scampered after Mary.

Mary walked across the yard to the work shed next to the farmhouse. She opened the door and waited for Manuel, and then stepped inside behind him. Mary placed the coffee and biscuits down on a side bench and walked over to where George was busily working.

"Good morning darling, you're off to an early start today so I bought you something to eat and drink," said Mary as she peered over George's shoulder. "How is everything going?"

"Your idea was right. I had enough scraps of leather left in the box. I am just about ready to see if it will fit," replied George.

Manuel tugged at Mary's skirt. He wanted to know what George was making. Mary bent down and gently picked up Manuel and placed him close to where George was working.

"Now my little friend. Let's see if this fits," said George
as he placed a little harness around Manuel.

"Oh George, it's a beautiful fit and matches the leather bag
I bought earlier," exclaimed Mary. George placed a mirror
in front of Manuel so he could admire his new harness.

Manuel was not sure about the new piece of attire, and he wriggled a bit to test it. When Mary placed him on the ground, he didn't need any persuasion and around and around he ran. Manuel was having so much fun with his new leather 'thing', he didn't notice George and Mary laughing. Mary picked him up again and placed him on the bench, where George removed the harness. "Looks like it fits Manuel," he said with satisfaction.

A few days later, Manuel noticed Mary packing a picnic lunch. *I can't remember the last time we went on a picnic* he thought excitedly. He sighed happily as Mary lifted him into his leather bag, picked up the picnic basket, and made her way to the garage, where George was waiting for them.

George placed the basket on the back seat,
made sure it was secure, then closed the door
for Mary and climbed into the driver's seat.

"Let's go," George said as they headed out of the driveway
and along the road toward the distant mountains.

As Manuel sat in his bag on Mary's lap, he watched the scenery that passed by. There were many tall trees, bridges, streams, and paddocks with sheep, and at other times, cattle grazing in the green fields. He loved spending time with George and Mary.

"Here we are," said George eventually, as he turned into a side road and stopped the car. "This looks like a good spot for the picnic." He gathered the picnic rug and basket and they walked to a shady tree where George spread the rug on the ground. Mary placed Manuel's bag on the rug, and then she sat down and unpacked the picnic basket.

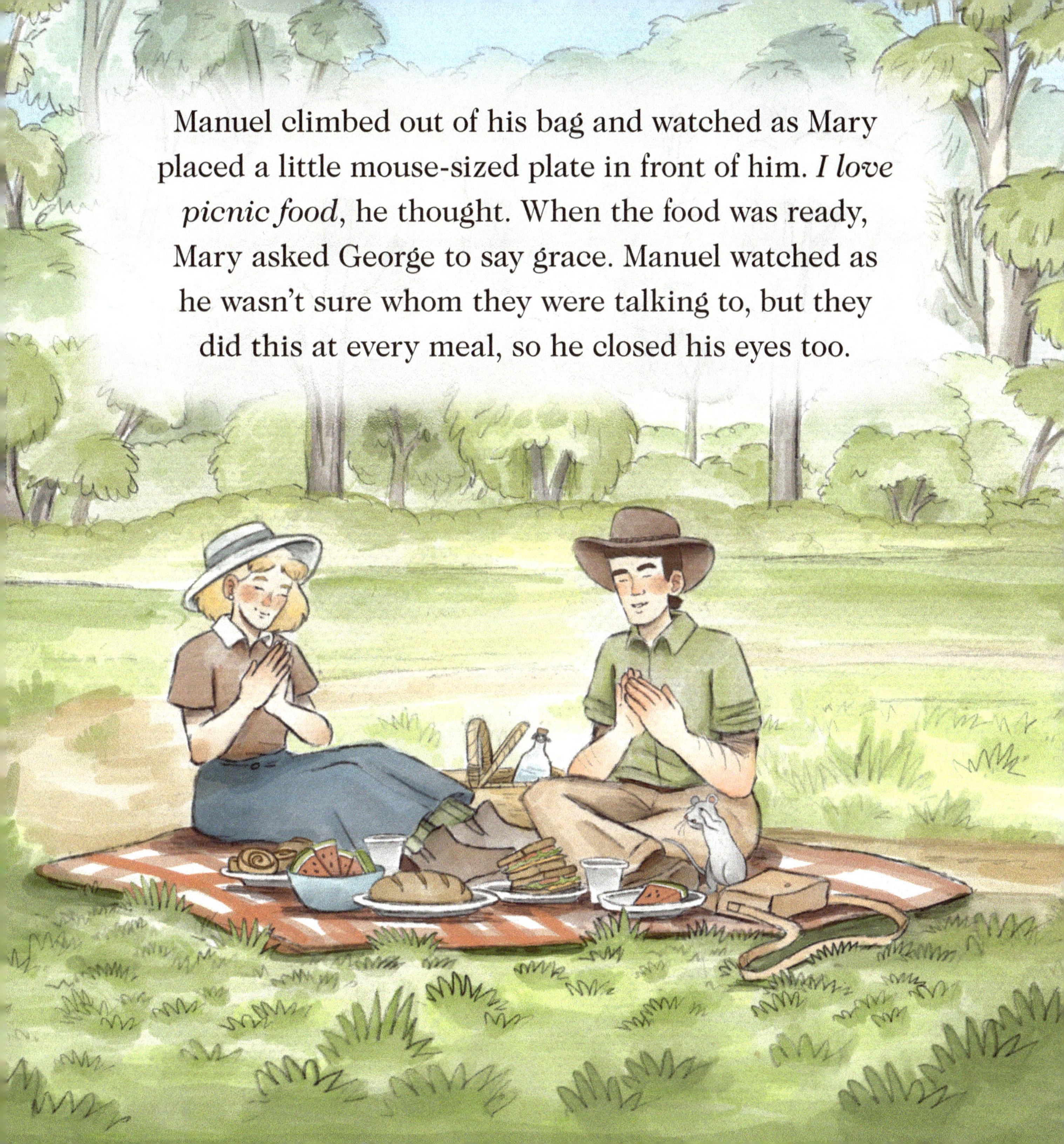

Manuel climbed out of his bag and watched as Mary placed a little mouse-sized plate in front of him. *I love picnic food*, he thought. When the food was ready, Mary asked George to say grace. Manuel watched as he wasn't sure whom they were talking to, but they did this at every meal, so he closed his eyes too.

George and Mary talked while they were eating.
Manuel nibbled the delicious food on his plate; Mary
had provided his favourite: CHEESE. Satisfied, he lay
back on the rug and watched the clouds go by. George
rested too until Mary said, "George if you're going for
a bush walk, you'd best head off soon. I'll clean up."

George thanked his wife and made his way to the
utility, picked up his backpack, placed it on his
back, tightened the straps and waved goodbye.

As George made his way up the track and out of sight,
Mary reached into the picnic basket and took out the little
harness George had made especially for Manuel.
He scurried to Mary and eagerly waited for her to place it
on him. Mary packed away all the plates and leftover food,
then placed the basket on the back seat of the utility.

Mary returned with something in her hand. Bending down she ever so gently attached a lead to the harness Manuel was wearing. Manuel remembered that Max had a harness and lead when George took him for walks. *We're going for a walk!* thought Manuel and he jumped up excitedly.

Mary began to walk and Manuel followed. While he allowed her to guide him, he knew no harm would come to him. It was easy walking along the river track. The trees towered ever so high over the little mouse. They almost looked like they had reached heaven.

They had not walked too far, when Mary said, "Let's go over there." They came to a lovely patch of thick grass. Manuel jumped and played as the grass was so soft and spongy. George always kept the lawn around the farmhouse short and well-mowed. The cows and sheep ate their grass. But this grass was different; so pleasant, that Manuel wished he could stay here forever.

Manuel exhausted himself playing and rolling in the grass and he finally stopped to rest. Mary laughed and said, "Come along my little friend. Let's get you a drink." *That's a great idea*, thought Manuel. Together, they continued down the path, as Mary guided Manuel with the lead.

It wasn't long before they came to a cool mountain stream. The water was crystal clear and looked so inviting. Mary lifted Manuel close to the edge so he could drink, and held him firmly. The tank water back on the farm was refreshing, but this water was crisp and cool and made his tongue tingle.

When Manuel had finished drinking, Mary placed him further back up the bank. "Are you ready for a little more adventure?" she said and smiled at Manuel. Manuel was always up for an adventure, so he began to stride ahead.

They proceeded down the bush track to a place where the trees parted and they could see blue sky, dotted with white clouds. Mary held the lead firmly and guided Manuel to a large rock.

"Look at that view," Mary said
as she led Manuel onto the rock.
From here they could see out over
the valleys to distant mountains
that appeared to go on forever.

*I've never seen anything like this
before*, he thought, trying to take in
everything that was before him.

Minutes passed and Mary looked at her watch and said, "It's time to go back Manuel, we've been here twenty minutes."

Manuel looked startled, *it seems like we've been here for hours*, he thought.

Manuel gave her a reluctant look, but then turned and began walking back along the bush track.

As they walked, Manuel looked up and saw giant stags growing in the tall trees. Many birds were flitting from branch to branch, calling to each other as they played follow the leader.

Manuel stayed close to Mary when he heard rustling in the bushes, only to see a scrub turkey run awkwardly along the track in front of them, then dart into the bush and disappear. He chuckled; he was always safe when Mary was nearby.

All too soon, they arrived back at the picnic spot. "Hello," Mary called as George appeared from his bush walk. George placed his backpack in the back of the utility and then folded up the picnic rug.

Mary gently took the lead and harness and placed
a weary Manuel in his leather bag.

"It seems a shame to leave our beautiful place. Goodbye
for now," said Mary as they all once again took their
places in the utility for the drive home.

As George drove, Mary told him about the sights and things they had seen on their way to the lookout. "I saw you from the top of the mountain, you looked so tiny," said George. Manuel was nowhere to be seen as he was curled up in the bottom of his leather bag and was sound asleep.

They arrived back at the farmhouse as a sleepy-eyed
little mouse poked his head out of the leather bag.
Mary carried him inside and placed him gently on his
blanket. "Good night, little friend." Manuel just lay there
as he thought about the day and his wonderful journey.

We all love to go for drives in the car or have a picnic in a park. It is also good to walk through the bush and look at the trees and bushes, birds and animals God has provided for our enjoyment. While we need to be careful as we walk, and where we tread, our parents will make sure we are safe.

Jesus wants to walk with us as we live each day. When we belong to Him, He will always take care of us. If you haven't asked Jesus to look after you, then why not do it now?

Notes to parents and carers

Children love to revisit their favourite stories. Each re-reading provides an opportunity to dig deeper into the text and reveal a fresh layer of meaning.

Manuel's Missions can be enjoyed in three ways:

- as simple children's narratives
- at a deeper level by making connections to our own lives and values
- concerning the teaching, David shared in the Bible.

Reading to young children (three to five years of age)

Initial readings should focus on the story and illustrations. Encourage the children to comment on the pictures and make connections to their own world, then ask:

- What did Mary say when Manuel arrived in the kitchen for breakfast?
- What did Manuel expect George to be doing when he went to the front verandah?
- Where was George this morning and what was he doing?
- How did Manuel react to the harness George made for him?
- Why do you think George made it? (Protection. Provision)
- What happened a few days later?
- Do you ever go on picnics and are they like Manuel's day out?
- Mary and Manuel worked hard to reach the rock. Their bushwalk was exhausting, but Manuel was rewarded when he saw the view. How do you think he felt looking at the view before him?
- What did the view and the things Manuel saw on the walk tell us about God's care for us?

Subsequent reading can focus on making connections to the child's own life:

- How should we react when dad or mum guides us and place restrictions on our activities?
- Can you list the things God has provided for us?
- How can we thank God for his provision?
- Remember to thank God for His care for us next time you go on a bush walk.

Reading to older children

In the Bible, Psalm 23:1-3, when King David was a young shepherd boy, he wrote these words. Read these verses to your child then:

In biblical times, the shepherd cared personally for his sheep, finding food, water, and shelter for them and protected the sheep from predators. When flocks mingled together, the shepherd called, and his sheep would follow his voice.

- Discuss the similarities between David's description of the shepherd in Psalm 23, and the story of *Manuel's Day Out.*
- Compare Mary and George's care for Manuel with the Father's love for us.
- Compare Psalm 23 and the story of Manuel's day out.
- Can you identify a message or common theme between the two?
  (protection, provision and restoration)
- What can we do to show our appreciation for God's provision for us?

Series titles available:

Book One	***The Servant Mouse***
Book Two	***A Cherished Place***
Book Three	***Manuel and the Spider***
Book Four	***A Mischievous Mouse***
Book Five	***Lost and Found***
Book Six	***Manuel's Day Out***
Book Seven	***Love One Another***
Book Eight	***Observations***

Books available from Manuel's Missions Facebook page, and www.wittonbooks.com

The Adventures of Max

The Adventures of Max Series is based on stories from the Bible and imparts valuable lessons to your children about their connection with God. Share in Max's Adventures on a small farm with his family George and Mary, and the many characters Max meets along the way. Each book is sold separately or collect the whole Series within Volumes 1 and 2, with the addition of Book 14, ***Reflections***, an Author synopsis of the Max Series.

Book One
The Defiant Mouse

Book Two
The Curious Chicken

Book Three
A Dog in Need

Book Four
An Old Friend Found

Book Five
The Rescue

Book Six
The Bush Fire

Book Seven
A Bad Influence

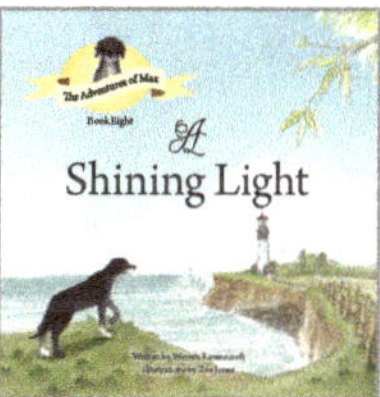

Book Eight
A Shining Light

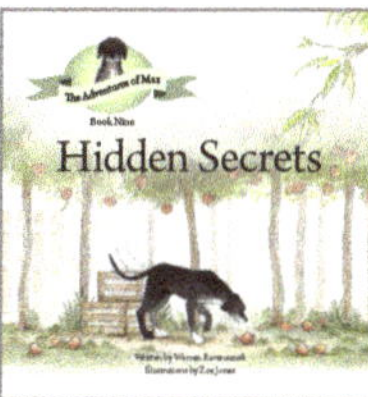

Book Nine
Hidden Secrets

Book Ten
A Foiled Plot

Book Eleven
Running the Race

Book Twelve
An Unexpected Reward

Book Thirteen
Max Welcomes a Friend

Book Fourteen
Reflections

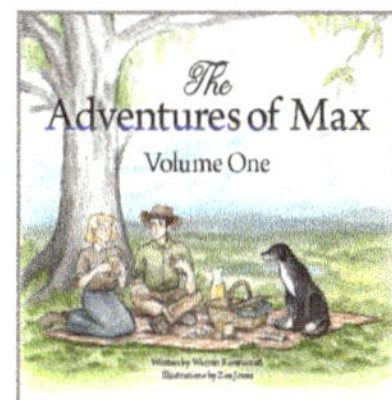

Volume One
Books 1 to 7

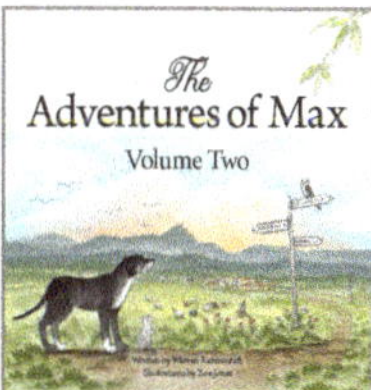

Volume Two
Books 8 to 13

Have you ever searched the four gospels to obtain the full account of Jesus life?

The Author, under their guidance of the Holy Spirit, took the words of the Apostle Paul to heart, when he wrote to Timothy and encouraged him to: "Study to show yourself approved unto God, a workman that needs not be ashamed, rightly dividing the word of truth".
2 Timothy 2:15.

The Life of Jesus
A Simple Narrative

In *The Life of Jesus - A Simple Narrative*, the author used language, similar to the New King James Version of the Bible to order and blend the four gospels into one complete story.

The Life of Christ
Simply Told

In the Second book, *The Life of Christ Simply Told*, the author used language, similar to the New International Version of the Bible to order and blend the four gospels into the complete story of Jesus life.

The Christmas Story, Retold

After attending a pre-Christmas church evening, I came away feeling numb due to the presentation of the Christmas story, by very secular people. Because I felt that some details of Christ's nativity had been misrepresented, I was led to write, *The Christmas Story, Retold.*

God, Man, Lucifer and the End Time

Is a collection of seven stand-alone documents. However, they all overlap and combine in a way only the Holy Spirit could implement. They are complex topics, requiring a great deal of study to 'bring it all together'. Prompted by the Holy Spirit and this work used as the 'foundation', may it lead to a greater understanding of the truth, majesty and love of our God.

Notes